Easy To Make And Use
LIBRARY
&
REFERENCE
BULLETIN BOARDS

by
Imogene Forte

Incentive Publications, Inc.
Nashville, Tennessee

Edited by Jennifer Goodman
Cover and illustrations by Susan Eaddy

Table of Contents

HOLIDAY AND SEASONAL

Preface

Want to beat the bulletin board blues? Here's the cure - an exciting array of creative bulletin boards that will have all your kids reading in no time! These new and exciting motivational bulletin boards are designed to encourage kids to read as well as to spruce up and add a spark of interest to libraries and classrooms. Each bulletin board has a specific focus whether it be holiday, seasonal, special interest or library know-how. Also included are complete instructions for colors, materials and construction plus a list of additional caption ideas and uses. Busy teachers, librarians and students will love these contemporary themed bulletin boards because they're easy-to-make, use and store and can be re-used year after year in many different ways. Patterns, ideas and captions can be combined to create new boards - all it takes is a little time, scissors, paper and staples. Altogether, the book offers 53 bulletin board designs with extra captions and combinations for over 250 different uses. Finally a bulletin board book for librarians and reading teachers that makes sense!

HOW-TO HINTS

Here are some suggestions to make the creation of your bulletin boards as simple as possible.

LETTERS

Materials: foil, yarn, string, newspaper, wallpaper, fabric, construction paper, ready-made letters

- Letters should be interesting and easy to read. They should contribute to the overall design of the board without being overpowering. In short, the letters should be large enough to be read easily but not so large as to take away from the other elements. If you feel comfortable doing it, try to design your own letters. Tearing the edges makes a nice effect or try cutting them out with pinking shears. Another alternative is to enlarge the letters given in this book on an overhead projector.

PATTERNS

- All patterns in this book will need to be enlarged. This can be done easily by using an overhead projector. To use an overhead projector, tape a large piece of paper on the wall and draw lines with a pencil. Then color the pattern with markers, paints, crayons or chalk. Or, cut the enlarged pattern into pieces and trace the pieces on appropriately colored construction paper. Laminating the patterns will make them last longer, enabling you to use them year after year.

BACKGROUND

Materials: wallpaper, fabric, tissue paper, wrapping paper, foil, newspaper, burlap, construction paper or butcher paper, cellophane, contact paper, shelf paper

- When making landscape backgrounds, try using 3 different shades of green paper. Cut 2 pieces slightly larger than necessary (see diagram) so that they can be overlapped for a more realistic effect. Use a light foreground, medium middle ground and darker background. By inserting the elements between ground layers you can begin to show perspective. Put large items in the front and progressively smaller items in the middle and back to add to this effect. Make clouds from paper, cotton or fiberfill.

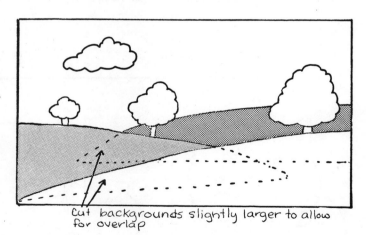

Cut backgrounds slightly larger to allow for overlap

DON'T FORGET TO

- Let students help. They love to be involved in the design and construction of their class bulletin boards.
- Use your imagination.
- Adapt any board to meet the needs of your particular classroom or library.
- Have fun!

SUGGESTED MATERIALS
- blue background
- black coat, hats, wand & bow tie
- yellow hair
- red table

- white rabbit
- red bird
- yellow stars

ADDITIONAL CAPTIONS
BOOKS ABOUT MAGIC
PULL A GOOD BOOK OUT OF THE HAT
READING IS MAGIC
THERE'S MAGIC IN A GOOD BOOK
ABRACADABRA!

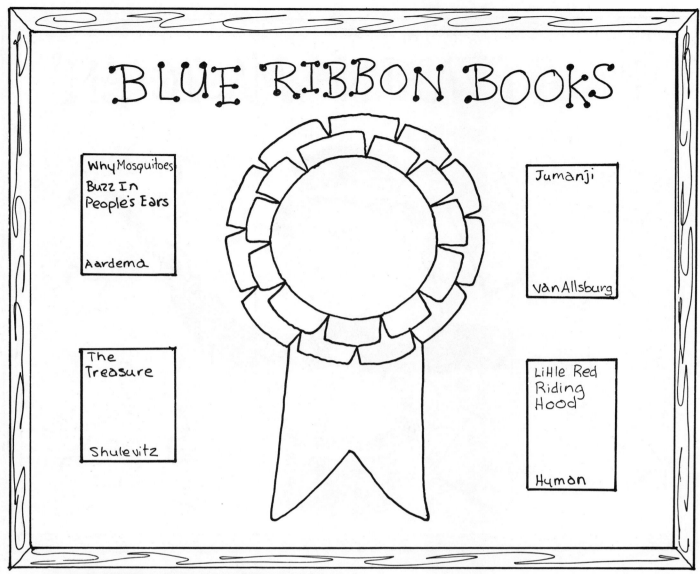

SUGGESTED MATERIALS
- blue ribbon
- gold background

CONSTRUCTION
Draw 3 circles from blue paper, each slightly larger than the last. Make 8 to 12 symmetrical cuts a couple of inches into the circle on the 2 largest circles. Pin the largest circle to the board. Place the medium sized circle on top of it and then the smallest circle in the center. Place the ribbon underneath all circles. Gently turn up the edges of the 2 largest circles for a 3-D effect. Place any message you like in the middle of the circle.

ADDITIONAL CAPTIONS
FIRST PLACE STORIES
BLUE RIBBON BIOGRAPHIES (Mysteries, etc.)
CALDECOTT WINNERS
TEACHER'S FIRST CHOICE (or Librarian's)

SUGGESTED MATERIALS

- pink background
- black cat
- lime green & purple swimsuit

CONSTRUCTION

Cut 3 long waves out of blue paper. Slip the book jackets in between.

ADDITIONAL CAPTIONS

JUMP INTO READING
WATER SPORTS
DIVE INTO AN ADVENTURE (Biography, Mystery, etc.)
DIVING FOR KNOWLEDGE

SUGGESTED MATERIALS

- blue background
- yellow butterflies
- green grass
- red tulips

- pink, yellow, blue & purple rainbow
- white bunny
- pink ears

CONSTRUCTION

Make the rainbow out of brightly colored tissue paper. Overlap the colors for a blended effect.

ADDITIONAL CAPTIONS

A RAINBOW OF READING
NEW BOOKS FOR SPRING
FOCUS ON EASTER
FIND THE POT OF GOLD AT THE RAINBOW'S END, READ

SUGGESTED MATERIALS
- use bright colors for hats & crowd
- pin actual hats to the board

CONSTRUCTION
Enlarge the crowd on an overhead projector and cut out as one piece. Have students color in the pictures using several bright colors. Hats may be drawn on or real hats may be pinned to the board.

ADDITIONAL CAPTIONS
GOOD BOOKS ARE A CROWD PLEASER
JOIN THE CROWD - AT THE LIBRARY
THE GANG'S ALL HERE! AT THE LIBRARY

SUGGESTED MATERIALS

- blue background
- white rabbits
- pink ears
- green grass

ADDITIONAL CAPTIONS

BOOKS FOR SPRINGTIME
GET THE RABBIT HABIT · READ A GOOD BOOK TODAY
PASS THE GOOD WORD! THE NEW BOOKS ARE HERE
WHISPER! A QUIET LIBRARY IS SPECIAL
EASTER OFFERINGS

Library Magic

Strega Nona
DePaola

The Velveteen Rabbit
Williams

Sylvester And The Magic Pebble
Steig

The Cat In The Hat
Geisel

The Silver Pony
Ward

SUGGESTED MATERIALS

- black background
- light purple robe
- yellow stars, moons & wand
- white letters for title
- light brown beaver
- white teeth
- black facial features

ADDITIONAL CAPTIONS

BE A READING WIZARD
THERE'S MAGIC BETWEEN THE COVERS OF THESE BOOKS
YOUR LIBRARY IS A MAGIC PLACE
THE WIZARD OF AHHS SAYS . . . READ

SUGGESTED MATERIALS
- lavender background
- green grass
- green & brown tortoises
- red feathers

ADDITIONAL CAPTIONS
JOIN THE TURTLE CLUB . . . READ BOOKS!
GET OUT OF YOUR SHELL . . . READ BOOKS!
THESE CRITTERS WON THE READING RACE, WILL YOU?

READING IS COOL!

SUGGESTED MATERIALS

- yellow background
- orange cat
- green sunglasses
- blue & green bathing suit
- red chair
- white glass with red & white straw
- pink lemonade in glass

ADDITIONAL CAPTIONS

COOL OFF WITH A GOOD BOOK
STRETCH OUT AND READ
SUMMERTIME FAVORITES

SUGGESTED MATERIALS
- white background
- blue water
- red letters

CONSTRUCTION
Provide students with a sailboat pattern. Ask them to decorate the boat and write on it the name of a favorite book.

ADDITIONAL CAPTIONS
TRIM YOUR SAILS WITH BOOKS
BOATING BOOKS
SAIL AWAY WITH SUSPENSE STORIES (Enlarge sailboat pattern and use only 3 or 4 along with several suspense story book jackets.)
SET SAIL WITH GOOD BOOKS
SAILOR'S CHOICE

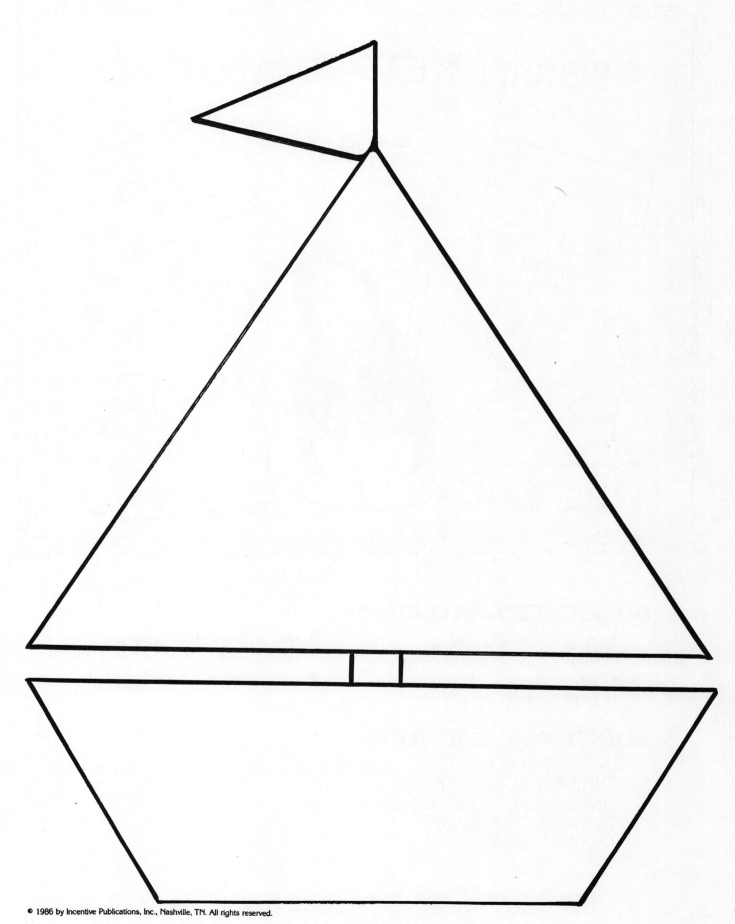

SUGGESTED MATERIALS

- yellow background
- black & white penguin
- pink pig
- blue overalls on pig
- red striped shirt on pig
- purple cat
- green dress on cat

ADDITIONAL CAPTIONS

HOORAY FOR BOOKS!
THE NEW BOOK PARADE
MARCHING FOR MYSTERIES
THE POETRY PARADE
AMAZING ANIMALS

SUGGESTED MATERIALS

- white background
- dark blue suit
- gold buttons
- pink cheeks
- black hat

ADDITIONAL CAPTIONS

DETECTIVE STORIES
READ ABOUT COMMUNITY
 HELPERS
SAFETY FIRST

SUGGESTED MATERIALS

- yellow background
- red hat, tights, sleeves & cheeks
- black feet
- red & black diamond pattern leotard
- white cotton balls for feet & hat

ADDITIONAL CAPTIONS

JUGGLE SOME GOOD
  STORIES
BOOKS THAT MAKE
  YOU LAUGH
A LAUGH A DAY KEEPS
  BOREDOM AWAY

These Books Are The Cat's Meow

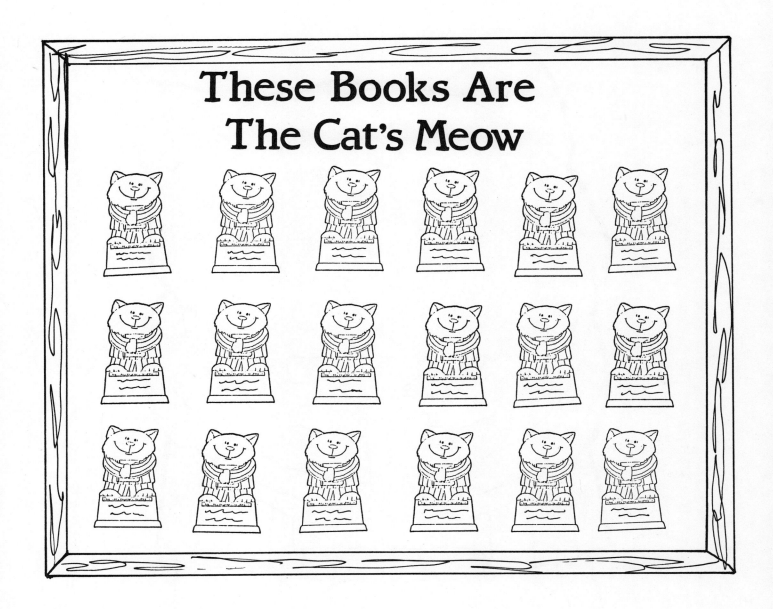

SUGGESTED MATERIALS
- green or blue background

CONSTRUCTION
Provide students with a cat pattern. Have them decorate the cat and then write on it the name of a favorite book. Display the cats on the board.

ADDITIONAL CAPTIONS
GOOD BOOKS ARE GRRRREEAAT!
NO KITTEN AROUND, THESE BOOKS ARE PURRFECT!
LOVE ME, LOVE MY CAT (animal story awards)
COOL CATS READ
SCAREDY CATS, COPY CATS AND OTHER CAT TALES

•THE CAT'S PAJAMAS TROPHY•

TIME TO READ!

Library Time
Free Reading

SUGGESTED MATERIALS

- pink or blue background
- gray clock
- black numbers & hands
- light pink or white face
- darker pink cheeks & lips
- yellow ring around face

CONSTRUCTION

Attach hands to the clock with a brad so that they can be moved.

ADDITIONAL CAPTIONS

YOUR TIME OR MY TIME - ANYTIME IS TIME TO READ
READ AROUND THE CLOCK
BOOKS ABOUT TIME

Welcome...
To A World Of Books

SUGGESTED MATERIALS

- blue sky
- 3 shades of green for grass & trees
- yellow sun
- red book
- black facial features
- yellow hands & feet

CONSTRUCTION

Use 3 different shades of green for the grass and trees. Use the lightest shade for the foreground, the medium shade for the middle and the darkest shade for the trees. Cut the middle ground and trees a little larger at the bottom so they can be overlapped easily. Place book jackets behind the hills.

ADDITIONAL CAPTIONS

ON THE ROAD TO GOOD READING
TRAVEL THE READING ROAD
BOOKS FOR KIDS ON THE GO

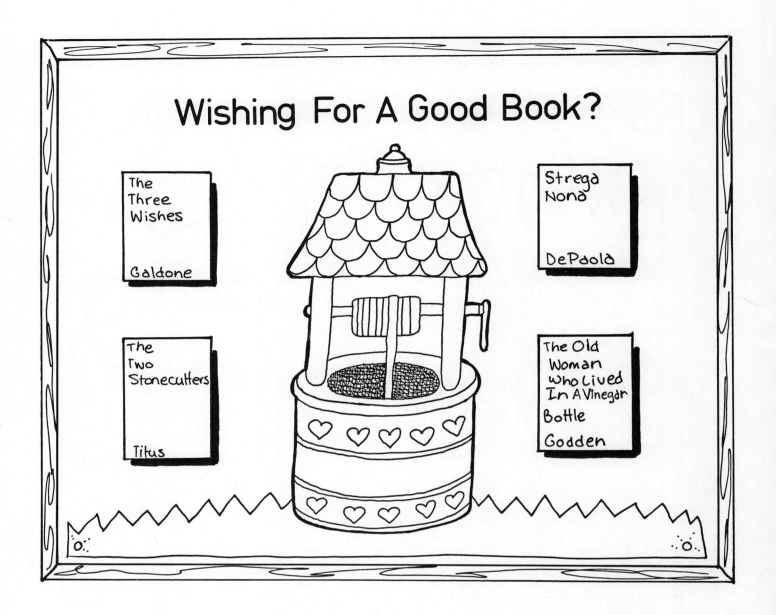

Wishing For A Good Book?

The Three Wishes — Galdone

Strega Nona — DePaola

The Two Stonecutters — Titus

The Old Woman Who Lived In A Vinegar Bottle — Godden

SUGGESTED MATERIALS
- blue background
- green grass
- white well
- red roof & hearts
- black hole

ADDITIONAL CAPTIONS
WISHES COME TRUE WITH A GOOD BOOK
READ ALL ABOUT FOUR WISHES THAT CAME TRUE
WISH UPON A GOOD BOOK
PULL UP A NEW BOOK

SUGGESTED MATERIALS

- white or yellow background
- red shirt
- blue pants
- blue & green globe
- black camera
- real filmstrip & cassette tape
- gray wrench
- brown shoes

CONSTRUCTION

Enlarge the elements on an overhead projector and color them accordingly.

ADDITIONAL CAPTIONS

HOW-TO-BOOKS
MR. FIX-IT SAYS READ!

Be A Winner!
Use The Card Catalog

SUGGESTED MATERIALS
- yellow background
- gray card catalog
- light brown bear
- red shirt & shoes
- blue pants
- white socks

ADDITIONAL CAPTIONS
THE CARD CATALOG "BEARS" LOOKING INTO
BEAR IN MIND · USE THE CARD CATALOG
IT'S A "BEAR-FACED" FACT · THE CARD CATALOG IS FASTER
 AND EASIER
LOOK IT UP
ARE YOU A CATALOG EXPERT?

DECODE THE DEWEY DECIMAL SYSTEM

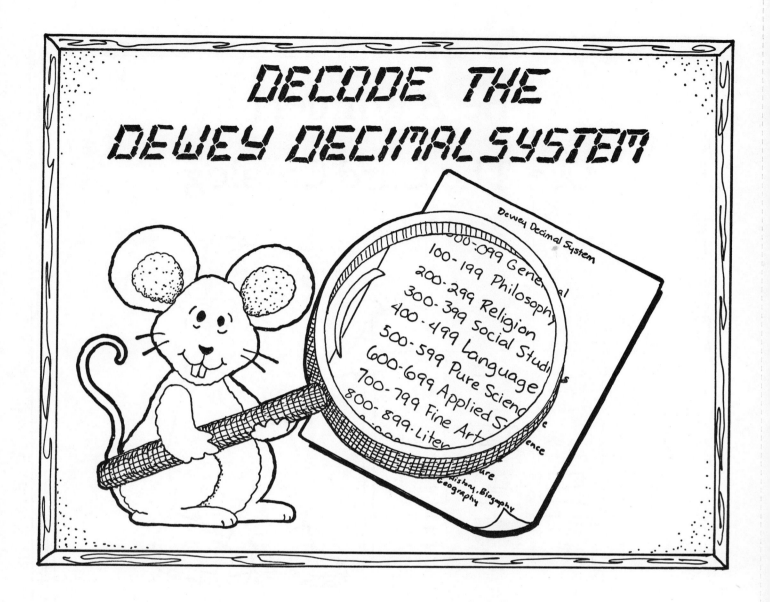

SUGGESTED MATERIALS
- pink background
- gray mouse
- black magnifying glass
- yellow paper

ADDITIONAL CAPTIONS
THERE'S SOMETHING FOR EVERYONE HERE!
BROWSE THROUGH A NUMBERED AISLE TODAY
YOUR GUIDE TO READING ENJOYMENT
DEWEY KNOWS THE WAY
LOST? ASK DEWEY
LIBRARY LINGO
DEWEY DID IT!

SUGGESTED MATERIALS

- black background
- dark green ground
- yellow stars
- orange fire with lighter orange or yellow inside

- yellow hair for girl & boy
- blue pants for both
- pink sweater for girl
- green sweater for boy

ADDITIONAL CAPTIONS

BOOKS ABOUT THE GREAT OUTDOORS
TALES TO TELL AROUND THE CAMPFIRE

SUGGESTED MATERIALS

- purple background
- green grass
- pink flowers with yellow center
- gray body
- white gown & cap

ADDITIONAL CAPTIONS

THERE'S BIG NEWS IN PERIODICALS

KEEP CURRENT WITH PERIODICALS

HIP, HIP HOORAY! THE NEW BOOKS ARE HERE

Name That Part

author
copyright page
cover
spine
title
title page
table of contents
illustrator
dedication

A Visit To
William Blakes
Inn

By Nancy Willard

Illustrated by
The Provensons

A Visit To
William
Blakes Inn

by Nancy
Willard

Illustrated by:
The Provensons
HBJ

For Ralph
who built the
Inn, & for Eric
who loves
Blake

Text copyright 1980
Illustrations copyright
1990 Library of congress
ISBN-PS3154 .00

Contents
12
14
16
18
20
22
24
26

SUGGESTED MATERIALS
- purple background
- gray kitty
- pink dress
- yellow list

CONSTRUCTION
Reproduce the actual pages from a book to pin on the board.

ADDITIONAL CAPTIONS
KNOW YOUR PARTS
THERE'S MORE TO A BOOK THAN MEETS THE EYE
FROM COVER TO COVER

Newbery Name Game

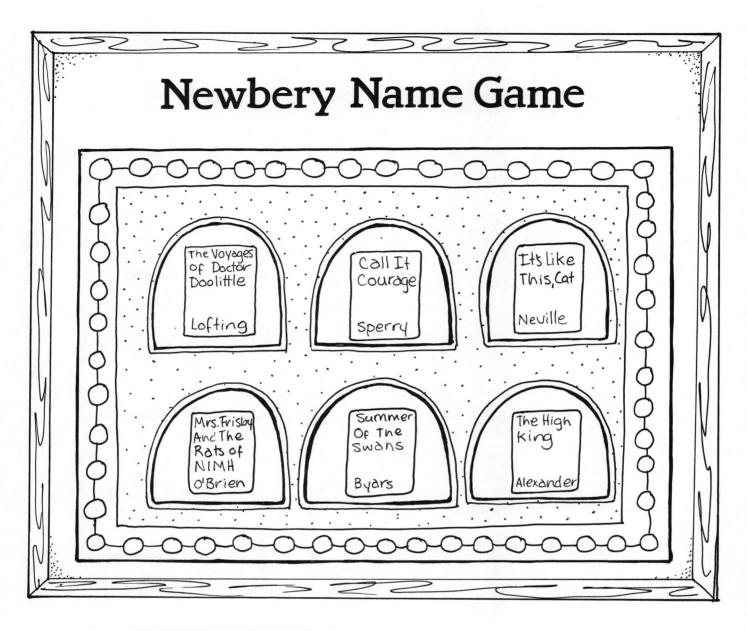

SUGGESTED MATERIALS
- pink background
- turquoise frame
- purple inside of frame

CONSTRUCTION
Use Christmas tree lights (blinking preferably) around the frame. Cut out windows.

ADDITIONAL CAPTIONS
NAME THAT AUTHOR! (Write names of books in windows.)
NAME THAT BOOK! (Write authors' names in windows.)
STAR SEARCH 1986!
CELEBRITY CIRCLE (Have kids draw a picture of their favorite
character from a book.)

SUGGESTED MATERIALS
- blue or black background
- white coat
- brown hair
- red tie

CONSTRUCTION
Have students write prescriptions explaining how certain periodicals can cure common classroom diseases. (Example: boredom, lack of knowledge, etc.)

ADDITIONAL CAPTIONS
Rx FOR READING
DR. GOOD BOOK SAYS . . .

RIDING HIGH ON REFERENCE BOOKS

Almanac · Atlas · Reader's Guide · Dictionary · Encyclopedia · Thesaurus · Rhyming Dictionary

SUGGESTED MATERIALS

- blue sky
- white cloud
- green bushes & grass
- red bird
- brown bear
- dark blue & yellow striped shirt
- black & white bicycle
- all different colors for books

CONSTRUCTION

Use 3 contrasting colors of green for the background. Place darker green bushes on the board and then overlap the ground in front of it.

ADDITIONAL CAPTIONS

WHEEL UP TO A WONDERFUL BOOK
THE BRIDGE TO LEARNING

Roll On References

SUGGESTED MATERIALS

- gray roads
- blue background
- 2 shades of green for hills & trees
- black tires
- brown tree trunks
- pink, orange, purple, blue & red trucks

CONSTRUCTION

Cut the hills from 2 shades of green paper. Put the darkest color in the front. Make the back hill slightly larger at the bottom so the front hill can overlap. Cut trucks and trees out separately. Place them on the road and hills.

ADDITIONAL CAPTIONS

10-4 GOOD BUDDY! THESE BOOKS ARE GREAT!
CAREERS IN TRANSPORTATION!
JOIN THE KIPLING CONVOY (Display books by Kipling)
JOIN THE CLEARY CONVOY (Display books by Cleary)

SUGGESTED MATERIALS

- red background
- green grass
- yellow giraffe
- white sign
- brown bangs
- yellow legs with brown spots
- black hoofs

CONSTRUCTION

Use white paper to make the sign. Write the rules on the paper with brightly colored markers. Change the message as indicated by the additional captions given below.

ADDITIONAL CAPTIONS

BOOKMARK BONANZA (Ask students to design and decorate bookmarks.)
LITTLE LIBRARIANS (Display pictures of students on the board.)
WHO WROTE IT? (Write book titles on the sign. Have kids find the authors.)
LIBRARY CALENDAR (Put monthly calendar on the board where the sign is. Note special dates.)
OLD FAVORITES (Have students write down names of favorite books.)
SPECIAL ANNOUNCEMENTS

RULE REVIEW

Library Rules

1. Use quiet voices

2. Put books on the book cart when finished with them.

3. Return books on time

4. Use bookmarks

5. Use the card catalog when looking for books

SUGGESTED MATERIALS

- blue background
- green grass & leaves
- brown tree trunk
- red tent
- white face
- yellow hair

ADDITIONAL CAPTIONS

CAMP OUT WITH A GOOD BOOK
BOOKS FOR SUMMER READING
NATIONAL BOY SCOUT WEEK
OUR NATIONAL PARKS
BOOKS FOR THE GREAT OUTDOORS

SUGGESTED MATERIALS

- yellow background
- red shirt
- blue pants
- brown shoes
- gray floor
- green drips & puddle
- blue, red & green paint cans
- real paintbrush
- student's painting

CONSTRUCTION

Use construction paper or real paint for the drips and puddle. Slide a student's painting under the artist's hand. Dab paint splotches on the girl with real paint.

ADDITIONAL CAPTIONS

READING PAINTS PICTURES WITH WORDS
BOOKS ABOUT FAMOUS ARTISTS
ART THROUGH THE AGES (art history books)

BE A FICTION FIEND!

SUGGESTED MATERIALS

- yellow feet & hands
- purple body, nose & ears
- pink face
- black background
- white sign with black lettering
- green cheeks & horns

CONSTRUCTION

Make a white sign and write FICTION FIEND on it. Use real string to attach the sign to the fiend. Draw on a smile. Cut white teeth from paper and attach. Insert book jackets under hands. When cutting out parts, add a little extra paper so the shapes can be easily overlapped.

ADDITIONAL CAPTIONS

MARVELOUS MONSTERS AND OTHER MAGICAL CREATURES
BELIEVE IT OR NOT?
GOBBLE UP A GOOD BOOK!

SUGGESTED MATERIALS

- light blue background
- brown spy coats
- purple pants
- black shoes
- brown & black floor
- brown hats
- yellow hair for girl spy
- orange hair for boy spy
- real magnifying glasses
- several different colors for pictures on the wall

CONSTRUCTION

Make a brown rectangle for the floor. Cut out two planks. Put black construction paper behind the floor. Put book jackets in the missing floorboards, the girl's coat pocket and behind the pictures.

ADDITIONAL CAPTIONS

FIND A GOOD BOOK AT THE LIBRARY
MAGNIFY YOUR MIND WITH READING

BEWITCHING BIOGRAPHIES

SUGGESTED MATERIALS

- white background
- black hats & cauldron
- purple dresses
- yellow stars
- green cheeks
- orange hair
- orange & yellow flames

CONSTRUCTION

Use orange construction paper to make the flames. Put a smaller flame made out of yellow construction paper inside the orange one.

ADDITIONAL CAPTIONS

HALLOWEEN STORIES
SCARY MYSTERIES
BREW UP A TALL TALE
BOOKS: THE MAGIC POTION

SUGGESTED MATERIALS
- black background
- yellow moon, stars & flames
- white spaceship with red, white & blue trim

ADDITIONAL CAPTIONS
UPWARD BOUND WITH A NEW BOOK
SCIENCE HISTORY IN THE MAKING
LAUNCH YOURSELF INTO READING
BOOKS ABOUT SPACE
EXPLORE NEW WORLDS WITH A GOOD BOOK

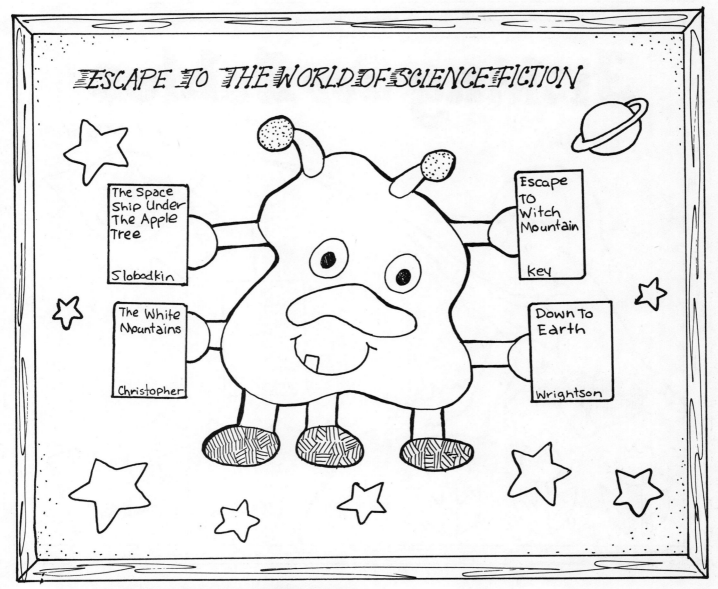

SUGGESTED MATERIALS

- black background
- yellow stars & planet
- green Martian
- black smile
- pink nose, hands & feet
- pink & yellow antenna
- white eyes with black dot
- white tooth

CONSTRUCTION

Cut pink circles for hands. Place book jackets on them. Draw on a black smile.

ADDITIONAL CAPTIONS

MONSTER STORIES
WHAT'S NEW IN SCIENCE
SPACE AGE SECRETS
MONSTERS, GIANTS AND OTHER AMAZING CREATURES
YOU'LL NEVER GUESS HOW THESE BOOKS END

SUGGESTED MATERIALS

- light blue sky
- green grass
- dark blue water
- yellow sun
- pink tulips

- dark green tulip leaves
- brown hair
- red shirt
- blue pants
- brown fishing pole

ADDITIONAL CAPTIONS

SUMMERTIME READING
NEW BOOKS FOR SPRING
I'D RATHER BE READING
DON'T LET THE BEST BOOKS GET AWAY
VACATION FAVORITES

SUGGESTED MATERIALS

- light blue background
- white cotton clouds
- pink or lavender dragon

ADDITIONAL CAPTIONS

BOOKS ABOUT MAGICAL CREATURES
DON'T BE DRAG-IN', PERK UP WITH A BOOK
HIGH FLYING READERS
FACT OR FICTION?

SUGGESTED MATERIALS

- black background
- yellow stars
- dark green grass
- yellow hair
- gray telescope
- red shirt
- blue pants
- brown shoes

ADDITIONAL CAPTIONS

ZOOM IN ON A GOOD BOOK
A UNIVERSE OF GREAT
    STORIES
TRAVEL THROUGH THE
    UNIVERSE WITH BOOKS
GAZE AT THE STARS OF
    THE WEEK
EXPAND YOUR MIND WITH
    READING
FOCUS ON FICTION
THIS MONTH'S LIBRARY
    STARS
THE SKY'S THE LIMIT

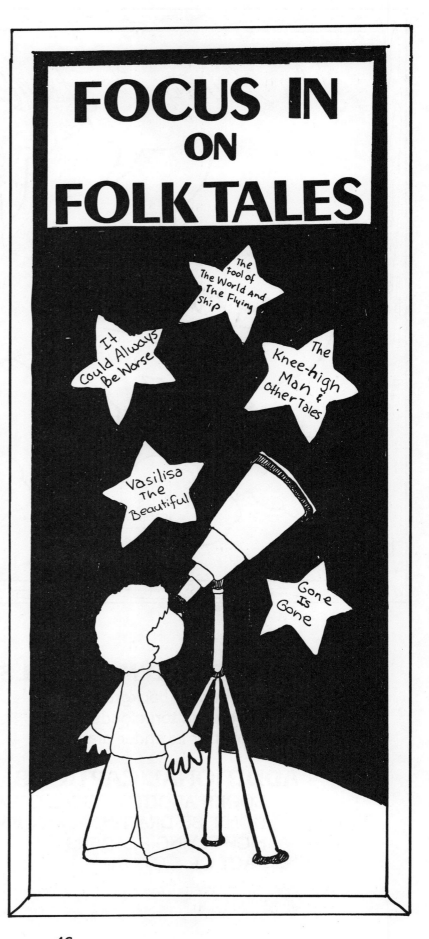

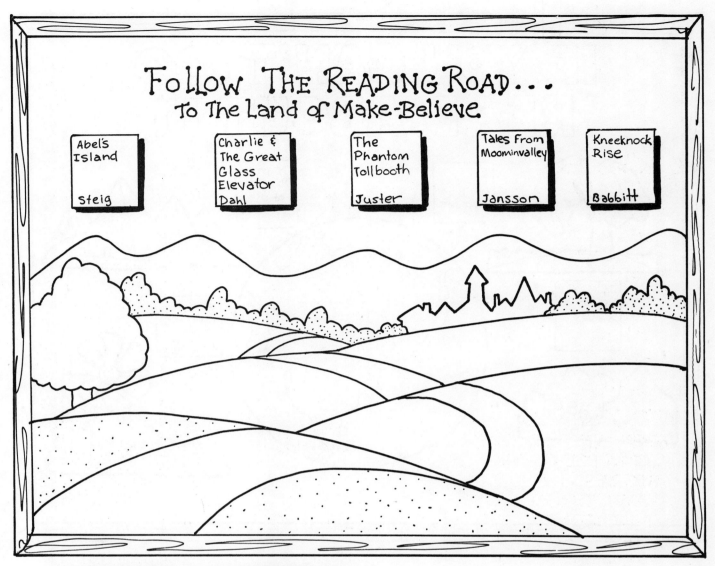

SUGGESTED MATERIALS

- blue background
- gray road
- purple mountains
- white town
- green grass & trees

CONSTRUCTION

Use 3 shades of green for the grass. Put the darkest in the foreground, medium in the middle and the lightest in the back. Overlap the pieces. Use medium green for the tree and brown for the trunk. Make background trees out of dark green. Have students draw fantasy figures to place along the road.

ADDITIONAL CAPTIONS

NEW BOOKS . . . COMING SOON
BOOKS ABOUT TRAVEL
TRANSPORTATION UPDATE (add book jackets or reports with truck and car backings)

SUGGESTED MATERIALS
- white background
- blue & green globe

CONSTRUCTION

Enlarge the pictures and color with markers. Or, substitute actual pictures, postcards, posters or magazine pictures of different places around the world. Students may prefer to make their own pictures by illustrating the setting of a particular book that they have read. Display book jackets beside the pictures.

ADDITIONAL CAPTIONS

TRAVEL TO FARAWAY LANDS
GEOGRAPHIC GEMS
IT'S A SMALL WORLD . . . UNLESS YOU READ
READ YOUR WAY AROUND THE GLOBE

SUGGESTED MATERIALS

- red wall
- brown or gray floor
- black notes
- black & white penguin
- yellow beak

ADDITIONAL CAPTIONS

STRIKE UP THE BAND FOR LIBRARY WEEK
STRIKE UP THE BAND FOR GOOD READERS
NOTE THESE NEW ARRIVALS
CONDUCT A SYMPHONY OF READING
TUXEDO TALES

SUGGESTED MATERIALS
- yellow background
- brown owl
- orange beak & feet
- white or light blue glasses

ADDITIONAL CAPTIONS
IT'S WISE TO READ
WHOO'S TOO BUSY TO READ?
TAKE A NEW LOOK AT YOUR LIBRARY
TAKE A NEW LOOK AT THESE OLD FAVORITES
WISE OWLS READ
NATURE STORIES
WHO-O-O DONE ITS?

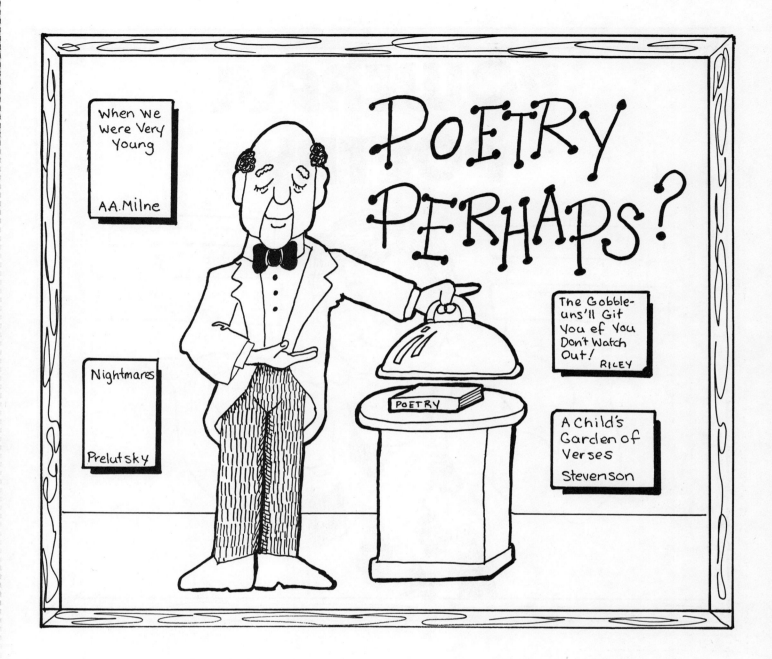

SUGGESTED MATERIALS

- pink wall
- gray floor
- black tie & pants
- white coat
- gold server
- purple book

ADDITIONAL CAPTIONS

PRESENTING POETRY FROM (class name)
FOR YOUR READING PLEASURE
POETS UNDERCOVER
SERVE UP A GOOD BOOK
GOURMET READING
GOOD READING . . . WELL DONE
TASTY BOOKS . . . NO CALORIES

POWERFUL POETRY

All the Day Long
The Scroobious Pip
The Moon is Shining Bright as Day
The Complete Nonsense Book

Listen, Children, Listen
Prayers From The Ark
Humorous Poetry for Children
The Bat Poet

SUGGESTED MATERIALS
- green background
- several different colors for books
- black hair
- black & brown shirt

ADDITIONAL CAPTIONS
HEAVY-WEIGHT BOOKS
BOOKS ABOUT ATHLETES
GET INTO SHAPE WITH HEALTH BOOKS
READING IS POWERFUL

SUGGESTED MATERIALS:

- red wall
- gray table
- white & blue beakers on table
- orange hair on scientist
- white lab coat
- purple beakers in scientist's hand

CONSTRUCTION

Make a gray rectangle for the table. Place the scientist behind the rectangle. Enlarge the other objects and color with markers. Place them on the table, overlapping for a nicer visual effect.

ADDITIONAL CAPTIONS

READ TO FIND OUT
IT'S NO SECRET · SCIENCE SUCCEEDS
WHY?

SUGGESTED MATERIALS

- black background
- brown radio
- red rug
- blue nightgown
- yellow hair

CONSTRUCTION

The rug, radio and girl can all be cut from separate pieces of paper and then overlapped on the board.

ADDITIONAL CAPTIONS

SHERLOCK HOLMES WEEK
RADIO PERSONALITIES
BEDTIME STORIES
THERE'S MYSTERY MAGIC IN YOUR LIBRARY

SUGGESTED MATERIALS
- white background
- red or green letters

CONSTRUCTION
Provide an elf pattern for each child or let them trace and cut out their own. (See pattern on next page.) Instruct the students to recommend a favorite book by writing the name of the book on their elf in the space provided. Then have them decorate the elves and display on the board.

ADDITIONAL CAPTIONS
LITTLE BOOKS TELL BIG STORIES
FAIRY TALES
ELFIN NOTES
WISHING YOU A MERRY CHRISTMAS
THE ELFIN WISH LIST

Gobble Up Good Books

Pilgrim Thanks-giving

Hays

I sailed on The Mayflower

Pilkington

The First Year

Meadowcroft

The Thanks-giving Story

Dagliesh

SUGGESTED MATERIALS

- yellow background
- cream colored head
- black lower body
- brown upper body
- orange beak & feet
- red wattle
- bright, contrasting colors for tail

CONSTRUCTION

Slightly bend the ends of the tail feathers for a 3-D effect.

ADDITIONAL CAPTIONS

THANKSGIVING TREASURES
STRUT YOUR STUFF . . . WITH GOOD BOOKS
DON'T BE A TURKEY . . . READ!
TURKEY TALES AND OTHER THANKSGIVING STORIES

Pumpkin Patch Publications

SUGGESTED MATERIALS
- an old pair of pants, a shirt, gloves & socks
- rope
- small pillowcase or paper bag
- straw or yarn

CONSTRUCTION
Stuff a pair of pants, a shirt, gloves and socks with newspaper. Tie the shirt sleeves, pants legs and pants with rope. Pin to the board. Use a stuffed paper bag or small pillowcase for the face. Draw on the features with markers. Stuff yarn or hay into the straw hat. Provide each student with a pumpkin pattern. (see page 59) Ask them to write a brief description of a favorite book on the pumpkin. Display on the board.

ADDITIONAL CAPTIONS
PICK OF THE PATCH
HALLOWEEN FAVORITES
THE ___ GRADE ISN'T SCARED OF THE LIBRARY

SUGGESTED MATERIALS
- yellow background
- green trampoline
- red or brown fox

ADDITIONAL CAPTIONS
JUMP FOR JOY · IT'S TIME TO READ
HOORAY FOR BOOKS!
BOOKS ABOUT SPORTS
FOXY FAVORITES

SUGGESTED MATERIALS

- orange, yellow & red leaves
- blue background
- red sweater & shoes
- green pants
- yellow hair

CONSTRUCTION

Have children make and decorate fall leaves for the bulletin board using the patterns given. You may want to have them write on the leaf the name and author of a favorite fall book to recommend to other students. Real leaves can be used instead.

ADDITIONAL CAPTIONS

* LEAF THROUGH A BOOK OR TWO
AUTUMN ADVENTURES
READ FOR KNOWLEDGE - USE YOUR LIBRARY

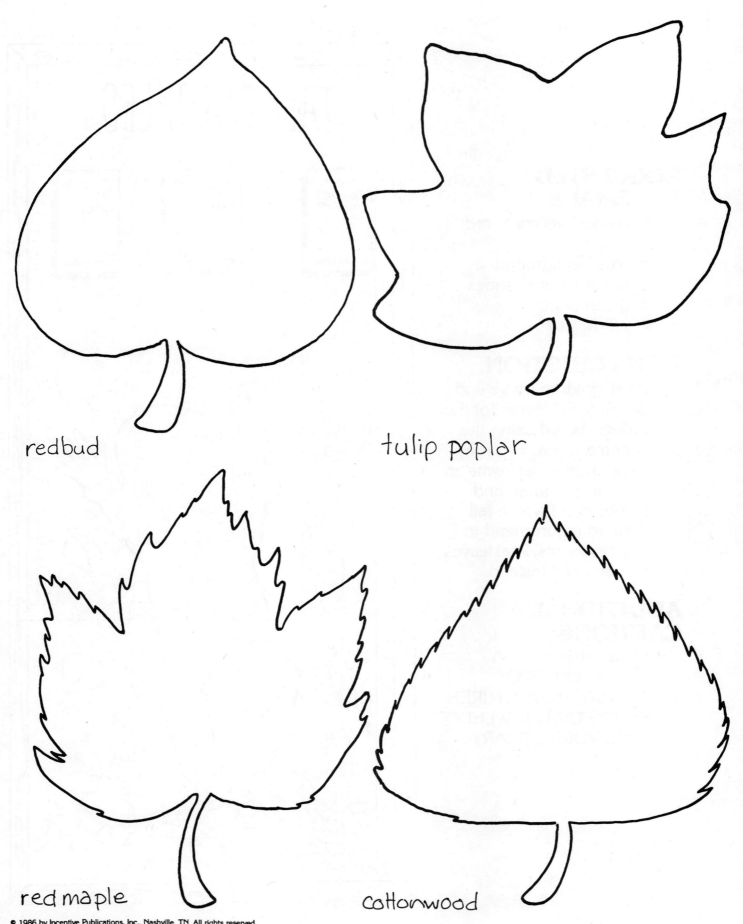

redbud

tulip poplar

red maple

cottonwood

Three Cheers For Summer Reading !!!

Alexander & The Terrible, Horrible, No Good, Bad Day
Viorst

Willaby
Isadora

A Bargain For Frances
Hoban

SUGGESTED MATERIALS

- green background
- gray swing
- yellow dog
- orange hair on boy
- blue shirt
- red shoes

CONSTRUCTION

Make paper chains out of gray construction paper. Attach them to the swing.

ADDITIONAL CAPTIONS

SWING INTO READING
LAZY DAYS ARE MADE FOR READING
EVEN PUPPY DOGS LIKE TO BE READ TO
PET STORIES

VALENTINES FOREVER

Peter &
Veronica
Sachs

Fifteen
Cleary

Ellen
Grae
Cleaver

I
LOVE
BOOKS

Bridge
To
Terabithia
Paterson

SUGGESTED MATERIALS

- light brown bear
- pink ears, nose & feet pads
- light blue background
- red valentines
- white doilies

ADDITIONAL CAPTIONS

YOUR LIBRARY JUST MAY HOLD YOUR HEART'S DESIRE
BEAR UP! THESE BOOKS WILL HELP YOU SOLVE YOUR STUDY
  PROBLEMS
BEAR"Y" GOOD BOOKS
PICK A HEART AND READ